Côora

Êfira ru carkigaã ye
diga ru carkigaã ye

Sugun

«Cessire sugun
kege» amma-i fatigi.

Kubbeyinere nusugi.
Ŋila 45 wugi.

Kûila môfuna
dûrugi.

Ini diga cûu dîre ginna
ru mire owon.

3

Zîŋki

«Agafur
bênoo
zîŋka
Alla-i
royiŋi.»

4

Zîŋki mire yîni bussu wugi. Zîŋka mura captuntu fora ru mureyintigi.

Zîŋka kîñila hunaã 23. Amma gura kîñili turon nu addi ŋa «zîŋki bôtii» intigi.

Malumaŋa

Côoru malumaŋa jôkuri aũ kege dîiŋa jillan nu amma-i «côoru amma» intigi.

6

Êruũ kûila hunaã daa yîsoo aŋkiruũ-i ini êruũ wugaã burayi gurti ceŋi.

Êruũ mire ini tra mire ŋa cîrigire burayiŋoo giri tirii kege duru direre warigi.

Tirii fîroo ina ariya kaga na irridoo lau dîi cîru wugi.

Kûm

Kûm mire fûrumtinne ru tai huma saga ceyinere ini saga ciiŋa rayiŋi.

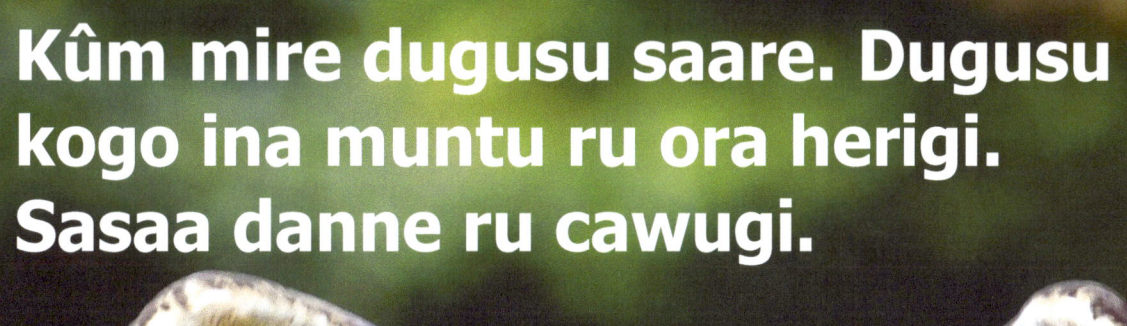

Kûm mire dugusu saare. Dugusu kogo ina muntu ru ora herigi. Sasaa danne ru cawugi.

Kûm mire woga-i dutoo fuyintigi.

9

Ômumur

Ŋili tigisoo
ômumur dau ŋûlli
dînere cirigi.

Yala hunaã eke kolokolom duro dûrugi.

Wortogo womoo kolokolom cî huma jakiŋi. Kolokoloma aga curunne ru yim tômu kûila daa buzugi. Aŋkiruũ maaši burayi gurti ceŋi.

11

Êlii

Côora duro êlii jasar
ni saa šilli ni.

12

Eke soli tarigi šilli aũ gûro daa bîinne kege na daa kûila hunaã dûrugi.

Ini tra jebici dîyoo turkona hunaã ru cubbu dîi goyi terigi.

13

Belebele

Yege huma eke daa kîkirciŋoo giskei kilakiŋi.

14

Yege ŋûlli ru dompere cî huma giskei ceŋi.

Foktintire yega huntaã muntu fora ru dompugi.

15

Tirkagelifi

Ini tra mire ŋa
cîrigire dunnoo
êfira ru yercinni.
Tafu daa tiganigi.

16

Yî dîiŋa ru surroki cîgi, dau kôlinne ru girciŋi.

Wire hinoo duro ciiŋa sowunni. Kûila cûu dûrugi, muntu dûnni.

17

Koro

Koro maaši huntuũ
amma fî burayintigi.

Aŋkira yega huntaã mura-i dompugi.

Êruũ kûila aguzuu ru goyi ni fôu na ga gor dûrugi.

Kûila kokinere digisa 15 tigisoo boyintire yala hunaã yercintigi.

19

Am-kûrei

Am-kûrei diga hunaã durusa. Yî bu hinnoo cawunni, duro tiganigi.

Bî wîni yerciŋoo am-kûrei ina kiruũ wayintu aga curukaã ginna wugi.

Am-kûrei yala ari-a addiyã hakiŋoo wugi.

21

Wogo

Wogo mire munafug. Ina zunta buru gisigi.

Wogo mire ôncol. Ini zuntu gisigire kogo môguruũ bênne gor hanayiŋi. Awini ini mire cîrigaã hanayiŋi.

Wogo kûila hunaã kokune ôwura cûu tigisoo, te ru sîgi mura burantu wirigi.

23

Êlikila

Êlikila firi huma yarka dîi. Kûsur huma êlli na dîi maru na dîi. Êfira hunaã zira zira.

Susur huma addira wogo ŋa ru cirigi.

Adani kogo auzudirigire burayiŋi.

25

Eke-totokti

Eke-totokti
eke cî ru
wawugi.
Ši bazinni.

26

Tiliši durusu dîi.

Ekaã duro ini tra kuili kege hakiŋoo tiliši huma durusu duro dînu goyiŋi.

Saa minikti kancinne ru 20 gor du wawugi.

Am-curulo

Am-curulo mire êbibi ŋa
fuyinere kukukinii ru dîi goyiŋi.

Aŋkala hunaã dîi. Ini mire ru cussu hanayiŋi. Êruũ kûila hunaã bûrru kuru-u kege lôyinere duro dûrugi.

Êbibi lau dîyoo eke ru wawire ele huma na giru yîgi huma bî cenere lili tigisoo êski ru wugi.

29

Eyer-lîfi

Aŋkiruũ tai huma ru goyi
ni kûnci huma na ga
yesku. Cî huma na maru.

30

Ina huna wuga
burayiŋaã hinoo
mire zuntu gisinni.

Kûila huntaã daa tuwai wôu ye
belke wôu ye êruũ daa yîsigi.
Dîski kogo aŋkiruũ daa yîsigi.

31

Capir

Côora duro šiya huna fušintigaã, capir. «Kûm šiya dîi, capir yaya dîi» intigi.

Saa hunaã šilli ciiru gûro nunukinni, tai huma meyinere rayiŋi.

Yege hun geyinni. Yege wogo-u walla ziŋki-u walla êlii-u hakiŋoo yala hunaã duro dûrugi.

33

Gûlei

Gûleya mura
ina addiyã
addiyã kuila
kaga wirigi.

Walla yîski warigi walla kiri warigi dêri kogo bussunni, tiganitii ciki ina wirigaã burayintigi.

Gûleya gura addira zîŋki bôtiĩ tûrutu cii.

35

Amma geyintiraã: APE ©2017
Amma ruyintiraã: Arumi Mamar, Mamar Bokor, Yîsip Ger and Rivers Camp (Galmai Wûji)
Aũ kêliyima: Robert Johnson (Sûmpi Zen)

ASSOCIATION

POUR LA PROMOTION

D'EDUCATION

www.ingramcontent.com/pod-product-compliance
Lightning Source LLC
Chambersburg PA
CBHW040307010626
45792CB00025B/1453